THOMSON
COURSE TECHNOLOGY
Professional ■ Trade ■ Reference

OpenGL® ES Game Development